Fact Finders®

~ DISGUSTING HISTORY ~

The TERRIBLE, AWFUL CIVIL WAR

THE DISGUSTING DETAILS ABOUT LIFE DURING AMERICA'S BLOODIEST WAR

by Kay Melchisedech Olson

Consultant:
John Derrick Fowler, PhD
Bandy Chair and Professor of History
Dalton State University
Dalton, Georgia

CAPSTONE PRESS
a capstone imprint

Fact Finders is published by Capstone Press,
1710 Roe Crest Drive, North Mankato, Minnesota 56003.
www.capstonepub.com

Library of Congress Cataloging-in-Publication Data
Olson, Kay Melchisedech.
    The terrible, awful Civil War: the disgusting details about life during America's bloodiest war / by Kay
Melchisedech Olson.
    p. cm. — (Fact finders. Disgusting history)
    Summary: "Describes disgusting details about daily life during the U.S. Civil War, including housing, food, and
sanitation" — Provided by publisher.
    Includes bibliographical references and index.
    ISBN 978-1-4296-3960-6 (library binding)
    ISBN 978-1-4296-6349-6 (paperback)
    ISBN 978-1-4296-8695-2 (saddle-stitched)
    1. United States — History — Civil War, 1861–1865 — Social aspects — Juvenile literature. 2. United States —
Social life and customs — 1783–1865 — Juvenile literature. I. Title.
E468.9.O476 2010
973.7′1 — dc22
                                                                                    2009026030

Editorial Credits
Christine Peterson, editor; Alison Thiele, designer; Wanda Winch, media researcher;
    Eric Manske, production specialist

Photo Credits
Abraham Lincoln, Draft of the Gettysburg Address: Nicolay Copy, November 1863; Series 3, General
Correspondence, 1837–1897; The Abraham Lincoln Papers at the Library of Congress, Manuscript Division
(Washington, D. C.: American Memory Project, [2000-02]), 4 (Gettysburg Address); CORBIS/Royalty-Free, 4 (Robert
E. Lee); CORBIS/Royalty-Free, 15; CORBIS/Timothy H. O'Sullivan, 21; Image courtesy of Gallon Historical Art,
Gettysburg, PA., www.gallon.com, 18; iStockphoto/Duncan Walker, 5 (Confederate flag); Library of Congress,
4 (Abraham Lincoln), 5 (U.S. flag, Surrender at Appomattox), 7, 17 (top), 23 (top) , 24-25 29 (top); North Wind
Picture Archives, 14, 27; Nova Development Corporation, 5 (factory, cotton); Painting by Don Troiani, www.
historicalimagebank.com, cover, 11, 12–13; Rick Reeves, Tampa, FL., 8–9; Shutterstock/akva, 17 (bottom), 23
(bottom), 29 (bottom); Shutterstock/freelanceartist, (design element throughout); Shutterstock/Turi Tamas, 11, 15, 18,
27 (design element); www.historicalimagebank.com, 6, 13 (top right), 20, 25 (surgeon's kit)

Primary source bibliography
Page 17 — from *Downing's Civil War Diary* by Alexander G. Downing and Olynthus Burroughs Clark
    (The Historical Department of Iowa, 1916).
Page 23 — as published in *Doctors in Blue: The Medical History of the Union Army in the Civil War* by
    George Worthington Adams (New York: H. Schuman, 1952).
Page 29 — from *Reluctant Witnesses: Children's Voices from the Civil War* by Emmy E. Werner
    (Boulder, Colo.: Westview Press, 1998).

Printed in the United States of America in North Mankato, Minnesota.
072012
006857R

TABLE OF CONTENTS

THE UNITED STATES DURING THE CIVIL WAR
1860–1865

PAGE 6
PAGE 16
PAGE 19

LEGEND

▬	UNION AND CONFEDERATE BOUNDARY
	FREE STATE
	SLAVE STATE
	U.S. TERRITORY
✸	BATTLES
	CAPITAL CITY
▥	CIVIL WAR PRISON
△	PLACES OF IMPORTANCE

N
W E
S

NOVEMBER 1860
Abraham Lincoln is elected president.

FEBRUARY 1861
Confederate States of America is formed; Jefferson Davis is chosen CSA president.

APRIL 12, 1861
Fort Sumter attacked; the Civil War begins.

SEPTEMBER 17, 1862
Battle of Antietam

JULY 1-3, 1863
Battle of Gettysburg

U.S POPULATION, 1860

FREE PEOPLE – 27,489,561

SLAVES – 3,953,760

CIVIL WAR DEATHS
(1861-1865) – 620,000

CONFEDERATE GENERAL ROBERT E. LEE
"It is well that war is so terrible, lest we should grow too fond of it."

PRESIDENT ABRAHAM LINCOLN
"Government cannot endure permanently half slave and half free."

NOVEMBER 19, 1863
Lincoln delivers his famous Gettysburg Address.

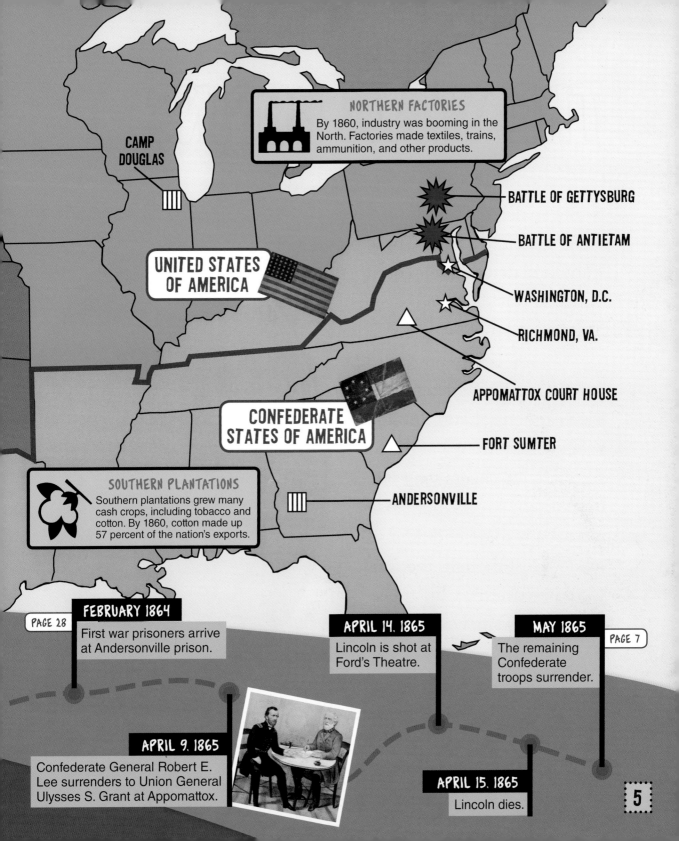

NORTHERN FACTORIES
By 1860, industry was booming in the North. Factories made textiles, trains, ammunition, and other products.

CAMP DOUGLAS

BATTLE OF GETTYSBURG

BATTLE OF ANTIETAM

UNITED STATES OF AMERICA

WASHINGTON, D.C.

RICHMOND, VA.

APPOMATTOX COURT HOUSE

CONFEDERATE STATES OF AMERICA

FORT SUMTER

SOUTHERN PLANTATIONS
Southern plantations grew many cash crops, including tobacco and cotton. By 1860, cotton made up 57 percent of the nation's exports.

ANDERSONVILLE

PAGE 28

FEBRUARY 1864
First war prisoners arrive at Andersonville prison.

APRIL 14, 1865
Lincoln is shot at Ford's Theatre.

MAY 1865
The remaining Confederate troops surrender.

PAGE 7

APRIL 9, 1865
Confederate General Robert E. Lee surrenders to Union General Ulysses S. Grant at Appomattox.

APRIL 15, 1865
Lincoln dies.

THE WAR BEGINS

During the U.S. Civil War (1861-1865), eager young soldiers marched off to fight for Union or Confederate armies. These proud men wanted to defend their countries. But army life was filled with death, disease, and foul living conditions.

The war began on April 12, 1861, when Confederate troops fired cannons at Fort Sumter. When Union troops at the fort surrendered, cheers rang out in southern streets. Both sides were ready to defend their way of life. Most thought the war would be over by Christmas.

Northerners were quick to join the Union army. Pro-Union people favored a strong federal government. Most were generally opposed to slavery.

WOUNDED UNION SOLDIER

ATTACK ON FORT SUMTER, SOUTH CAROLINA

Southerners had opposed Abraham Lincoln for president. Southerners believed states' rights were most important and that slavery was a way of life. Lincoln's election started the **secession** of 11 states.

When the fighting ended in May 1865, weary soldiers returned home to a changed nation. Many men limped on a leg and a crutch. No one was ever the same again.

secession: the formal withdrawal from a group or organization, often to form a new group

TATTERED UNIFORMS

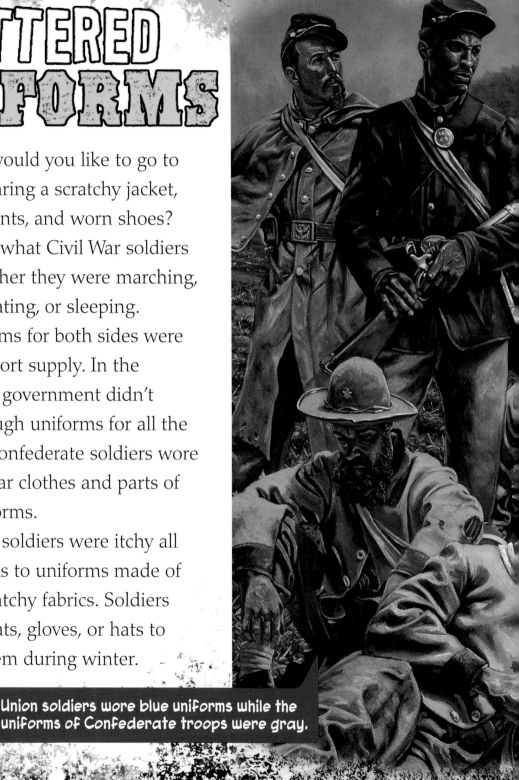

How would you like to go to school wearing a scratchy jacket, tattered pants, and worn shoes? That's just what Civil War soldiers wore whether they were marching, fighting, eating, or sleeping.

Uniforms for both sides were often in short supply. In the South, the government didn't make enough uniforms for all the soldiers. Confederate soldiers wore their regular clothes and parts of army uniforms.

Union soldiers were itchy all over thanks to uniforms made of rough, scratchy fabrics. Soldiers had no coats, gloves, or hats to protect them during winter.

Union soldiers wore blue uniforms while the uniforms of Confederate troops were gray.

Soldiers' uniforms quickly looked like dirty rags. Uniforms became stiff and stinky from sweat. Jackets and pants were ripped, dirty, and spotted with blood. Uniforms were rarely washed. Underwear? Soldiers didn't change or wash their underwear for months at a time. Soldiers seldom received replacement clothing, so they took jackets, pants, or boots off the dead.

Socks protected a soldier's feet. But a soldier's socks went unwashed for weeks or months. They soon became stiff and filled with germs. As the war dragged on, soldiers wore their boots with bare feet. When boots wore out, soldiers wrapped their feet in rags and kept on marching.

HARD GROUND, WET BEDROLLS

Sleeping outside might sound like fun to you, but for Civil War soldiers it was miserable. Little protected them from rain, snow, or summer heat. Even less protected them from pesky mosquitoes and body lice. Mosquitoes buzzed and bit all night long. Lice infested soldiers' bedrolls, clothing, beards, and hair.

Lucky soldiers slept in canvas tents with dirt floors. Other soldiers slept on the ground on bedrolls. These blankets were rolled up and carried on the soldiers' backs while they marched. If the ground was wet or if rain fell at night, bedrolls became soggy and muddy.

Crowded, filthy living quarters were great for bacteria and germs. Diarrhea was a common complaint for soldiers. They also suffered pneumonia, typhoid, cholera, and tuberculosis.

Civil War soldiers spent many cold nights sleeping outdoors on the ground.

FOUL FACT

Some soldiers slept in open-air beds made by piling hay or straw between two logs.

TEETH DULLERS

Think school lunches are bad? Try dining on stale, moldy crackers day after day. Hoping for some meat with your meal? Look closer at the crackers. Those small specks are maggots. Sound disgusting? Maybe so, but hardtack crackers were standard food for Civil War soldiers.

Hardtack was made from flour, salt, and water. It was light and easy to carry. The salt in hardtack helped soldiers to sweat, which kept them from fainting in the heat.

Hardtack crackers were called "teeth dullers" and "iron plate biscuits" because they were so hard. "Worm castle" was another name for hardtack because it often was full of weevils and maggots. Some soldiers dipped their hardtack in hot coffee to soften it and kill the worms. Others went ahead and ate the worms.

Meat was scarce for soldiers. Depending on what was available, soldiers ate the meat of cows, horses, mules, and even rats. Salt helped preserve meat. But often the meat was rotten.

HARDTACK

A diet of hardtack and salted meat left soldiers constantly thirsty. The water they drank came from nearby streams, ponds, and lakes. Drinking dirty water caused soldiers to develop **dysentery** and other diseases.

> **dysentery:** a sometimes deadly infection of the intestines that causes diarrhea

ON THE MARCH

Civil War soldiers did most of their traveling on foot. One Union soldier marched 143 miles (230 kilometers) in 16 days, with a two-day battle in between. That's a lot of ground to cover in worn-out boots, no socks, and blistered toes.

Soldiers marched 15 to 20 miles (24 to 32 kilometers) a day. But hot weather made long marches risky. Soldiers who wore wool uniforms and carried bedrolls, food, and guns often fainted when marching on hot days.

Weary from travel, soldiers marched into battle.

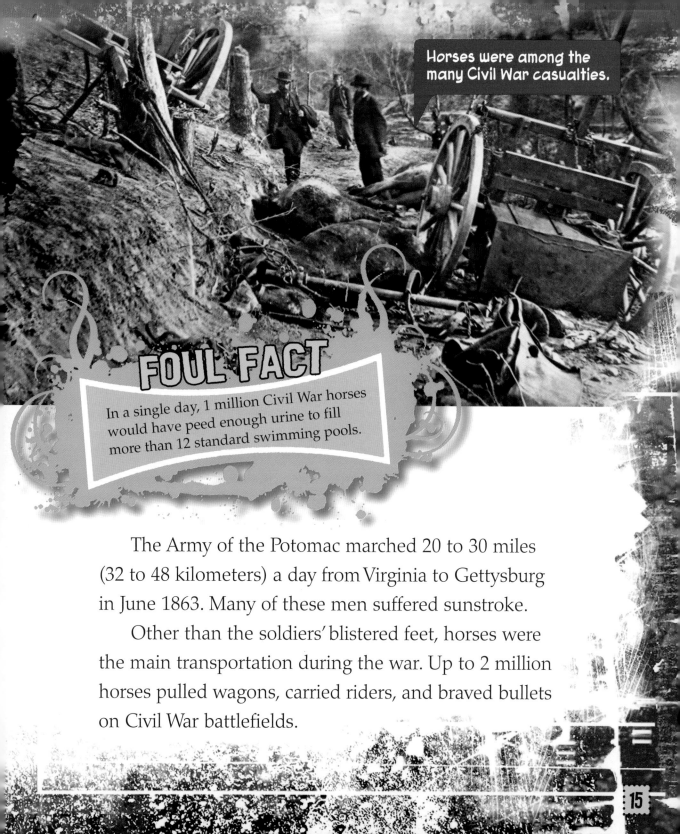

Horses were among the many Civil War casualties.

FOUL FACT

In a single day, 1 million Civil War horses would have peed enough urine to fill more than 12 standard swimming pools.

The Army of the Potomac marched 20 to 30 miles (32 to 48 kilometers) a day from Virginia to Gettysburg in June 1863. Many of these men suffered sunstroke.

Other than the soldiers' blistered feet, horses were the main transportation during the war. Up to 2 million horses pulled wagons, carried riders, and braved bullets on Civil War battlefields.

DEADLY WEAPONS

Why were the battles of the Civil War so horribly bloody? Civil War soldiers were armed with rifles. Rifles were accurate at much farther distances than past weapons. The newer weapons had a closer **range**. Their rifles shot lead bullets that exploded when they hit bone. But soldiers still had to advance near enemies to drive them off the battlefield. The closer the bullet's impact, the more damage it caused.

These rifles could crush an advancing enemy as they did during the Battle of Antietam. On September 17, 1862, in Maryland, Union soldiers marched shoulder to shoulder, creating a wall of men. Confederate soldiers, lying in a nearby cornfield, suddenly stood up and fired. Union soldiers went down in waves. Antietam was the bloodiest single day in the Civil War. Close to 23,000 men were killed, wounded, or captured.

range: the farthest distance ammunition can travel to reach its target

DEAD SOLDIERS AT ANTIETAM

Battle Wounds

Thomas Hains of Company E took off his hat, placed it on his ramrod, and holding it up, shouted to the boys along the line to see what a close call he had had while out in front, for a minie ball had passed through the creased crown of his hat, making four holes. Before he could get his hat back on his head, a small shell burst over us and mortally wounded him.

Sergeant Alexander G. Downing
Confederate Army
Sunday, April 5, 1862

FOUL FACT

Metal shells exploded in air. They rained down sharp pieces of metal, killing large numbers of soldiers.

Soldiers for both the North and South suffered heavy losses at Gettysburg.

Minie balls were the most common ammunition used. These lead balls caused about 108,000 battlefield wounds. Head shots killed instantly. Stomach shots were usually fatal too.

During the Battle of Gettysburg in July 1863, Confederate troops were mowed down by gunfire as they advanced during Pickett's Charge. Soldiers lay where they fell with large holes in their stomachs.

Arms and legs hit with minie balls were often **amputated**. Shattered bones could not be put back together. Wounded soldiers made a **tourniquet** from a belt, rope, or shirtsleeve to stop the bleeding.

If ammunition ran out, soldiers used bayonets at the end of their guns to attack the enemy. Bayonets sliced through uniforms. Germs from the dirty uniforms were plunged deep into the victim's body. Infected wounds killed many soldiers long after the battle.

amputate: to remove an arm or a leg

tourniquet: a tight wrapping designed to prevent a major loss of blood from a wound

BATTLING GERMS

Imagine being a Civil War soldier on the march for hours under a hot sun. Your stomach is churning. That bacon you ate last night smelled bad, but you ate it anyway. Now you feel like your guts might explode. At last the commanding officer shouts, "Take 10," and you rush to the nearest bush.

After, you hurry down to the pond below to wash. Then you take off your sweaty hat, fill it with pond water and drink. "Fall in," the officer shouts, and you march off again.

People were unaware of germs in the 1860s. Disease spread easily in war conditions. The sicker soldiers got, the worse their living conditions became. If soldiers washed at all, they did it in the same water they drank.

In the 1860s, some people, even doctors, believed that full beards protected men from sickness. But the opposite was true. Spit, vomit, and blood stuck to moustaches and beards. Lice often made their homes in the long beards.

A Confederate soldier's sewing kit included a toothbrush and washcloth.

Civil War soldiers often bathed in murky river water.

By 1863, living conditions for Union soldiers became so bad that generals began issuing **hygiene** orders. Men were ordered to wear their hair short and bathe twice a week. They were to change clothes at least once a week. But soldiers often ignored these orders.

hygiene: actions people perform to stay clean and healthy

PILES OF WASTE

Picture yourself living in a camp with hundreds of men and piles of waste all around. Pretty stinky, huh? During the Civil War, human and animal waste piled up around army camps, hospitals, and prisons. Keeping clean was an impossible task.

Union and Confederate soldiers dug trenches to use as latrines. These stinky dirt pits were often dug close to the camp's water and food supply. If the waste wasn't covered with a layer of dirt daily, flies became a serious problem. Flies feeding on waste brought germs to the camp food supplies. Rain washed the waste into the ground, where it mixed with the water supply.

Field hospitals were almost as bad as the camps. These temporary hospitals were set up in tobacco storehouses, animal barns, large tents, or even in the open air. Doctors and nurses seldom washed their hands between caring for the wounded men. When they did wash, it was often with water **contaminated** from nearby latrines.

contaminated: dirty or unfit for use

Surrounded by Waste

We find about the grounds, an area of over three acres, encircling the camp as a broad belt, on which is deposited an almost perfect layer of human excrement [waste].

A sanitary inspector, describing "Camp Misery," a camp for wounded soldiers in Alexandria, Virginia.

SAWBONES

For a Civil War soldier, the field hospital was more dreaded than the battle itself. These temporary hospitals were hastily set up near battlefields. Doctors often had few supplies and little or no clean water. Bare, bloody ground was the only bed for most of the wounded soldiers.

Civil War doctors treated soldiers for many illnesses. Diarrhea was the most common, and deadly, disease. More Civil War soldiers died from diarrhea than were killed in battle.

More than 70 percent of the patients treated had injuries to their arms or legs. Amputation was the most common treatment for wounded soldiers. Amputations were done with little or no **anesthesia**. Seriously wounded men in the field waited for hours, sometimes days, for treatment. Doctors stood for hours, sawing through bones. This method of amputation gave Civil War doctors the nickname "sawbones."

Union soldiers tend to a wounded man in 1861.

anesthesia: a gas or injection that prevents pain during treatments and operations

Doctors treating the injured did not know about bacteria and germs. They treated patient after patient without first washing their hands or their instruments. Civil War doctors wore bloodstained coats as they tended to patients. Bloody bandages and sponges used to wash wounds were rinsed out in buckets of dirty water and reused.

SURGEON'S AMPUTATION KIT

PRISON HORRORS

Life on the battlefield or in field hospitals was horrible. But nothing compared to the horrors suffered by prisoners of war. Men captured in or after a battle were sent to prison camps.

Camps were crammed full of prisoners. Sick and healthy men lived together in filthy conditions. Flies, bugs, maggots, and lice lived on the soldiers.

Starvation was a daily threat for prisoners. An army that could barely feed its soldiers cared little about feeding enemy prisoners. What food prisoners got was often unfit to eat. Food was simply dumped on the filthy ground. Prisoners fought each other for every scrap.

Beds were seldom provided for prisoners. Most men slept outdoors. They had nothing to protect them from the weather.

Lack of fresh fruits and vegetables led many war prisoners to get scurvy. Scurvy victims could not chew any solid food. Their gums became black and rotten.

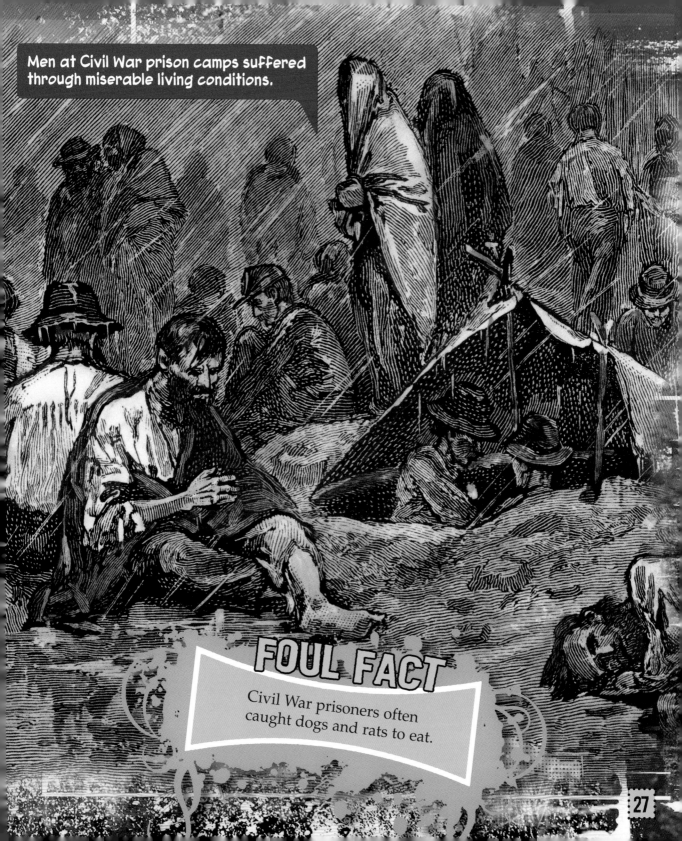

Men at Civil War prison camps suffered through miserable living conditions.

FOUL FACT

Civil War prisoners often caught dogs and rats to eat.

Outnumbered guards feared prison escapes. They allowed only a few inmates to go to the latrines at any one time. Many inmates waited two or more days for the chance to go. Prisoners lived in pools of their own waste.

The Confederacy's Andersonville is the most infamous of all Civil War prisons. In all, about 33,000 Union soldiers found themselves in Andersonville at some point during the Civil War. More than 13,000 men died at this camp in Georgia.

A wooden fence surrounded the camp, but it was almost unneeded. A line around the prison marked the boundary for prisoners. A single finger across this deadline was enough to get a prisoner shot on the spot.

But cruel treatment of prisoners was not limited to the Confederates. Camp Douglas in Chicago was considered the North's Andersonville. Hunger and disease plagued inmates here as well. To prevent their escape, prisoners were not allowed to wear clothes. Even blankets were taken away. Many Confederates imprisoned at Camp Douglas froze to death.

ANDERSONVILLE PRISON CAMP, 1864

Disease and Despair

There are millions and millions of all kinds of vermin here, flies, bugs, maggots and lice, some of them as large as spiders. If they once get the best of you, you are a goner. A great many of the prisoners are hopelessly crazy, starvation, disease and vermin being the cause . . . I am somewhat crippled, myself, but I manage to try and wash and keep clean, that is the principal thing. One hundred have died within the last 24 hours.

Michael Dougherty

Teenage Union Soldier imprisoned at Andersonville

May 1864

GLOSSARY

amputate (AM-pyuh-tayt) — to cut off someone's arm, leg, or other body part, usually because the part is damaged

anesthesia (a-nuhs-THEE-zhuh) — a gas or injection that prevents pain during treatments and operations

contaminated (kuhn-TA-muh-nay-tuhd) — dirty or unfit for use

dysentery (DI-sen-tayr-ee) — a sometimes deadly infection of the intestines that can cause diarrhea

hygiene (HYE-jeen) — actions people perform to stay clean and healthy

range (RAYNJ) — the farthest distance ammunition can travel to reach its target

scurvy (SKUR-vee) — a deadly disease caused by lack of vitamin C

secession (s-SESH-uhn) — the formal withdrawal from a group or organization, often to form a new group

tourniquet (TUR-nuh-ket) — a tight wrapping designed to prevent a major loss of blood from a wound

typhoid (TYE-foid) — a serious infectious disease with symptoms of high fever and diarrhea that can lead to death

READ MORE

Landau, Elaine. *The Battle of Gettysburg: Would You Lead the Fight?* What Would You Do? Berkeley Heights, N.J.: Enslow Elementary, 2009.

Mattern, Joanne. *The Big Book of the Civil War: Fascinating Facts about the Civil War, including Historic Photographs, Maps, and Documents*. Philadelphia: Courage Books, 2007.

McNeese, Tim. *Civil War Battles*. The Civil War: A Nation Divided. New York: Chelsea House, 2009.

Sheinkin, Steve. *Two Miserable Presidents: Everything Your Schoolbooks Didn't Tell You about the Civil War*. New York: Roaring Brook Press, 2008.

INTERNET SITES

FactHound offers a safe, fun way to find Internet sites related to this book. All of the sites on FactHound have been researched by our staff.

Here's all you do:

Visit *www.facthound.com*

FactHound will fetch the best sites for you!

INDEX